# Brush Brush Brush

By

**Sunday Treasures**

For your media interview and speaking engagements at

www.drreneesunday or www.drreneemd.com

For print information address Sunday Company at the

address below.

ISBN:

Library of Congress Control Number:

Published by:

Sunday Publishing Company

2890 GA 212, Suite 153

Conyers, Georgia

(786) 565-8199

www.sundaypublishingcompany.com

Hi there! I am Sam!

I like most things sharks do.
Like swimming really fast, or
splashing, or sleeping in the sand.

But do you know what else I like to do ?
Brush my teeth!

In the morning after breakfast

Then after lunch

And after dinner

I like brushing my teeth so much because I like having strong healthy teeth and a pretty white smile!

Sometimes the other sharks make fun of me for brushing my teeth, but I just ignore them. Because their teeth are nowhere near that pretty as mine!

And if they're not careful,
they'll get a lot a painful cavities.
And soon they may not even have teeth at all!

Hi Sam, we're sorry for making fun of you.

Do you mind showing us how to bush our teeth too?

Sure! Hey do you guys want to learn as well?

And make sure you get every single tooth!
Even the ones in the very back.

When you brush your teeth, make little circles like this!

Then once you're done brushing, rinse your mouth out with cold water.

Ooh! Ooh! And don't forget to floss! Flossing helps keep little pieces of food from geting stuck in your teeth and causing cavities.

Wow, thanks Sam!
We sure learned a lot!

You're welcome!
Now if you remember the steps
I showed you and brush your teeth
three times a day, soon you'll have healthy
sparkly white teeth like mine.

THE END

www.ingramcontent.com/pod-product-compliance
Lightning Source LLC
Chambersburg PA
CBHW040852100426
42813CB00015B/2778